YOUR KNOWLEDGE HAS VALUE

Bibliographic information published by the German National Library:

The German National Library lists this publication in the National Bibliography; detailed bibliographic data are available on the Internet at http://dnb.dnb.de .

Imprint:

Copyright © 2017 GRIN Verlag
Print and binding: Books on Demand GmbH, Norderstedt Germany
ISBN: 9783668706170

This book at GRIN:

https://www.grin.com/document/426226

Sarah Wunderlich

The Spark That Started a Fire. Annie Leibovitz's Iconic Image of Pregnant Demi Moore and Its Impact Until Today

GRIN Verlag

GRIN - Your knowledge has value

Since its foundation in 1998, GRIN has specialized in publishing academic texts by students, college teachers and other academics as e-book and printed book. The website www.grin.com is an ideal platform for presenting term papers, final papers, scientific essays, dissertations and specialist books.

Module M11: Intercultural Competence - Power, Ethics, Ideology: Photography and the Politics of Representation

SoSe 2017

Hand-in-date: 08/28/2017

The Spark That Started a Fire – Annie Leibovitz's Iconic Image of Pregnant Demi Moore and Its Impact Until Today

Sarah Wunderlich

Master of Education, Gymnasium

Mastersemester: 2

Semesters in total: 8

Table of Contents

The Spark That Started a Fire – Annie Leibovitz's Iconic Image of Pregnant Demi Moore and Its Impact Until Today

1   Introduction

Imagine seeing a naked and very pregnant woman on a cover of a fashion and/or lifestyle magazine while doing your weekly shopping. Coincidentally, the woman pictured is not only pregnant but also good looking at the same time and most likely, she is famous for something. Today, we are no longer surprised or even shocked by that cover, we are simply used to seeing beautiful, famous, naked, and pregnant women on magazine covers as the likes of Britney Spears, Natalie Portman, and Claudia Schiffer posed for them as did almost every otherwise famous woman being pregnant. Because somehow it seems to be good form in the world of celebrities to expose the growing belly. Consequently, it appears naturally as if it always had been common practice to put the pregnant body on display naked or scarcely covered, revealing more than concealing leading to "next-door women" to do just like celebrities do in social media.

But this has not always been the case. When Annie Leibovitz shot a series of photographs of Demi Moore in 1991, who at that time was seven months pregnant and had no difficulties in posing naked, covering her breasts only with her hands (see Appendix 1) and even published this photograph on Vanity Fair's August 1991 issue, the world seemed to have stopped for a minute. In an article by the New York Times on the iconicity the photo has reached in the past 25 years, Vanity Fair's editor in chief said:

> "I never questioned that I wanted to publish it. It seemed to me a wonderful celebration of the essence of womanhood," [...] "I knew that some would find it offensive, and indeed when our publisher Ron Galotti showed it to Walmart, they insisted that we had it shrink-wrapped or it would not appear on the newsstands. This just made it more X-rated." (Tavani par. 4).

This quote already hints at the explosiveness and uniqueness the photograph and especially the publishing of it had. Up to then, pregnant women were scarcely to be seen on magazine covers unless it were for medical representations (Nash 28). But in this case, Demi Moore was not pictured for the pathological condition of her body but to demonstrate her "cultural power and wealth and [her being] an idealized white woman" (ibid. 29). The pregnant body was no longer a de-sexualized object, constrained by taboos and myths as feminist scholars including Carole Stabile (193), widely agree upon.

Looking at changes this picture is believed to have triggered, it seems feasible to argue that it not only changed society towards a tolerant, embracing view on pregnancy but also initiated a process of objectivizing the pregnant female body to an extent, at which even during this physically demanding time, women strive to perfect their body. Additionally, women feel a growing pressure to look toned and shaped post-partum as if nothing has happened. Hence, they put their own body at the center of attention stepping away from old view of nurturing as their main duty to an extent of self-neglect.

In this paper I would like to discuss the abovementioned picture and its protagonists, look at the past perception of pregnancy and motherhood and illustrate the changes that evolved after the photograph was published. Thus, by illustrating the changes, the development and processes this "ground-breaking" (Leibovitz in Tavani par. 5) picture enabled should become obvious underlining the paper's thesis of the picture as being a step towards a more self-confident, physically attractive self-image of pregnant women but also becoming a trigger of pressure and excessive self-control.

2   The Photograph and Its Protagonists

The August 1991 issue of Vanity Fair, a magazine on popular culture, fashion, and current topics of interest, featured an unprecedented photograph on its title page. Being intended as the cover story to promote Demi Moore's upcoming movie, it pictured the actress wearing nothing but a huge diamond ring (Bellafante par. 2) looking quite alluring at the camera. The picture was taken in a way that nothing could distract the onlooker's view from the actress. The pregnant belly is positioned at the central but lower third of the portrait. Soft lightening was being used falling from an upper right angle on the actress's face and shoulders. While her face is illuminated quite well looking directly at the camera, her belly, being shown from the side only, blurs with the darker background of the image making it quite difficult to detect the actual boundaries or dimension of the belly. While covering her breasts with one arm, putting the enormous diamond ring on display, the other arm holds or hugs the belly, drawing additional attention at it. Apart from the ring, the image does not use any further accessories striving to purely depict Demi Moore's condition and put it at the center of attention. This is also underlined by the actress's minimalistic make-up, it appears as if she was wearing none, and hair style.

In 1991, Demi Moore was a very successful and well-paid actress starring in several box office hits (Biography, IMDb.com, par. 13). Not only has she been very open in the cover story, revealing details about her private life, she also supported Annie Leibovitz's idea to use this portrait shot of her nude and seven months pregnant for the magazine's cover (Leibovitz no page). According to the photographer, Demi Moore generally was not shy at having very private moments like the birth of her first daughter in 1988 accompanied by friends and professional photographers (ibid.). Furthermore, she is said to having been very self-conscious as she did not want any body make-up or post-editing of the shot (ibid.). But she also knew that she was working with one of the most successful portrait photographers at the time, Annie Leibovitz (Bellafante par. 2, Tavani par. 1) with an aptitude for iconic shots (McGuigan par. 3). Having worked for more than a decade at the Rolling Stone, she started working with Vanity Fair in 1983, already being known to shoot both "stunning and often controversial" images (Biography on Annie Leibovitz, par. 7). According to Leibovitz's recount, she and Demi Moore had worked together several times before (Leibovitz[1] par. 4). Initially, the cover photograph was not intended to be published but eventually, Leibovitz and the editor in chief at Vanity Fair came to the conclusion that this image would be the perfect picture for the occasion (ibid. par. 5). Although everybody involved knew that publishing this picture would cross a line, no one expected the reactions being so intense (ibid. par. 5). Leibovitz's straightforward portrait received wide-spread world-wide attention varying from expressions of disgust (e.g. letter to the editor in Stabile 190) and complaints that even pregnant women were now subject to sexual objectification (Leibovitz par. 2) to an appraisal of finally "assert[ing] a space for the pregnant body in the public realm as a complete detachment from the rules and regulations that govern the pregnant body with regard to body image, sexuality and status" (Nash 29). Moreover, the image was being discussed as evoking "Botticelli's Birth of Venus" (Siegel 257). Nevertheless, a wide audience was offended and the image provoked an unexpectedly intense debate for Vanity Fair summing up at "ninety-five television spots, sixty-four radio shows, 1,500 newspaper articles and a dozen cartoons" (Stabile 189).

---

[1] The excerpt quoted from is to be found in appendix 2 as the online version was no longer accessible.

In order to understand the reason for this vast upheaval it is important to understand how pregnancy and motherhood were perceived up to the early 1990s.

3 Perception on Pregnancy and Motherhood

From today's perspective the scandal the Demi Moore shot caused is no longer comprehensible. Being used to body-hugging maternity wear, magazines using picture of pregnant celebrities to boost their sales, and even the Average Janes[2] putting their pregnant bodies on display in social media, we no longer have to comply with social norms and standards that still prevailed in 1991. Following, I will root those norms and cultural constructs of pregnancy and motherhood back to the Victorian times and trace them to the late 1980s and early 1990s in order to discuss the fierce reactions the photograph provoked and later on the changes stemming from it.

3.1 History

"Throughout centuries and cultures motherhood has been guided and constrained by [...] world views espoused by a greater culture" (Bins and Dale 3).

Although this quote may vary in applicability it certainly can be seen as point to case during Victorian times. As the Victorian woman was "defined by her reproductive capacity" (Poovey 35) her individuality ceased to exist by the time she "became what she desired to be" (ibid. 52), a wife and mother. Even the Victorian law did no longer regard wives as individuals but as an extension of their husbands (ibid.), while medical scholars, e.g. W. Tyler Smith, saw no more than the uterus in women, to which they associated crucial value to society overruling female individual interests (ibid. 35). Furthermore, the woman's "reproductive function defined her character, position, and value [...]" (ibid. 37) but at the same time, she needed control and surveillance (ibid.). As Stabile puts it, "pregnancy has been traditionally predicated on an essentialism that reduces women to passive vessels [...]" (192) suffering from various nervous conditions (Poovey 37). This basic difference from men required women to be constantly supervised. Moreover, in line with this view, childbirth was marked as a disorder (ibid.).

After having given birth, the Victorian image of a mother being the 'Angel of the house' (Poovey 8) dominated a woman's life. Caring and nurturing were regarded as the

---

[2] Average Jane as a synonym for common, non-famous, and average women.

6

prime tasks for women, who, as partially described above, had to have no other interests due to her passiveness. This take on motherhood defined how mothers have been portrayed throughout history: a good mother was the one who was "saint-like", humble, and gentle, putting herself and her interests always last (Birns and ben-Her 47). Furthermore, society increased the pressure by asserting that "good mothers produce good children" (ibid. 57). Summarizing, mothers or mothers-to-be are no longer an individual but subordinated to self-neglect and nurturing due to their gender (Robinson and Stewart 862). So, being a woman the overall aim was to becoming a wife and mother and thus, turning into a medical pathology (Nash 28) ruled by cultural construction. The self was no longer of importance and the societal rules to being a good mother and a decent mother-to-be were to be followed. "The ideal female 'reproductive citizen' was expected to place her children's health and well-being above her own needs and desires" (Lupton 2).

Surprisingly, this argumentation still prevails in the 20th and even 21st century with Fraiberg climaxing it with the claim that mothers have to be the primary care givers to their children, who in in her view are entitled to full-time care in order to raise them to "good children" (ibid. 56). Fraiberg went even further in claiming that "the survival of the human race is [...] dependent on a mother's ability to provide" undistracted love, denying mothers of individual needs and interests (ibid.). Therefore, Fraiberg's arguments seem to be fueled by the Victorian view. The discussion or argument about whether a stay-home or working mom is the better mother is certainly stemming from this claim. And although we tend to think that Victorian times are a part of history for long time by now, I claim that the views made it into present times as well.

A survey by the Women's Media Action Group conducted in the early 1980s and looking at stereotypical representation of gender roles in media asserted that women were mainly pictured at home with the children (Lowe 23). Celebrity mothers were stylized as being good mothers if seven prerequisites identified by Douglas and Michaels were met: the mom had to be "gorgeous" with distinct ideas about her future (dedicated to mothering, of course), dearly and increasingly loved by her significant other. Furthermore, she is completely content with her role as a mother, delighted by being surrounded by her children, sporting the "maternal glow" and looking fabulous after birth (Douglas and Michaels in O'Brien Hallstein 17). Additionally, she is a fully aware eater who designs her nutrition according to the latest findings of healthy eating and is disciplined when it comes to work-outs (ibid.). With the closely observed Princess of Whales, those prerequisites were being worked through, labelling her as a good mother and idealizing her as a role model for the newly defined so-called 'momism' (ibid.), an ideology going beyond the Victorian idea of a good mother and enhancing it by the aspect of positive self-perception.

3.2 The Pregnant Body

With regards to the pregnant body, I would like to highlight three aspects that possibly contributed to the intense reactions the Demi Moore photograph evoked. Before discussing in which details the photograph clashed with prevailing perceptions on the pregnant body, they firstly need to be explained.

First of all, women seem to lose proprietary possession over their bodies once they are pregnant. Generally, the female body holds a place in a hierarchy "not of their own making" (Giovanelli and Ostertag 1) requiring permanent monitoring and upkeep (ibid.). Due to the assumption of women being passive vessels and thus need to be closely monitored, the pregnant body turns into an "object of medical scrutiny and surveillance" (Stabile 191). Moreover, the representation of the maternal body as dangerously permeable (Lupton 2) forces a mother-to-be to limit and control herself, constraining her entire life so that she adequately "manages her body" in order to protect the pre-born (ibid.). Shulamit Firestone elevates a pregnant woman's obligation to self-neglect and dispossession of her body to an even higher level by stating that "pregnancy is barbaric [...] [it] is the temporal deformation of the individual's body for the sake of the species" (Firestone in Stabile 192). Even law makers seem to agree with the opinion of dispossessing the pregnant woman of her body as they claim that the right of privacy "is not absolute" (Neff 328), ruling pre-born children as minors without a parent and posing as their guardians (Lupton 5). Furthermore, "bodily integrity [...] has not been extended to pregnant women" (Neff 328). This take on the pregnant body being subject to extrinsic forces rather than the woman's interest leads to the second aspect to be discussed, namely that a pregnant woman is no longer regarded as being an individual. This goes in line with the Victorian view on married women and takes the level of denying a woman of her individuality a step further. Interestingly, studies have shown that women felt as if "their own body has been taken over" once the social environment had found out about the pregnancy (Lupton 5). Moreover, as pregnant women

8

are still represented according to the Victorian vessel metaphor, they no longer feel as an individual with own needs and priorities (ibid.). This detachment of the female pregnant body from the individual seems especially in America quite paradox as the American culture has a highly individual trait in its culture which recedes in the light of the self-proclaimed child –centeredness of the American society (Birns and Dale 5).

Finally, a look at the perception of the pregnant body is necessary. Although media and society want to convey that "motherhood [and pregnancy] is easy, natural, and enjoyable" (Hoffnung 164) "the pregnant body – even clothed – is a source of abjection and disgust in popular culture" (Stabile 191). Not only is the swollen belly regarded as awkward, accompanied with the notion of discomfort and oftentimes seen as "grotesquely excessive" (Stabile 191), it is also in juxtaposition to the prevailing paradigm of slenderness (Nash 30) and it is always a reminder of sexuality (O'Brien Hallstein 85). As Gow ascertained in her study, weight gain during pregnancy, which is both unavoidable and essential, was portrayed as generally negative (Gow et al. 4). Furthermore, a pregnant body is absolutely not seen as being sexually attractive, more as being "aesthetically and culturally problematic" (ibid. 27). This is underlined by the account of Waverman stating that "maternity fashion was a little infantilizing and made every pregnant woman look enormous. The clothing looked like it was actively trying to erase any idea of sex from everyone's mind." (Waverman Blog). Consistently with this experience is the fact that the depictions of pregnant women was very limited in non-medical publications (and here certainly clothed) and for medical publications as illustration for pathology and medical interests. Moreover, pregnant women were never associated with any sexual desires when depicted (Nash 34). Thus, women were expected to adhere to society's expectations that pregnant bodies perform in certain ways in public and (preferably) stay hidden (Butler in Nash 37).

With these three aspects discussed, the loss of proprietary possession of a woman's pregnant body, followed by the dissolution of her individuality and the environments opinion of a pregnant woman's outward appearance and sexual attractiveness, the reactions on Demi Moore's photograph may become more comprehensible.

4 The Photograph's Impact

Demi Moore was a very successful actress in the late 1980s and early 1990s, earning enormous amounts as a guild's afemale agent (Biography of Demi Moore). Moreover, movies like 'Ghost' (1990), 'Mortal Thoughts' (1991) and later on 'Indecent Proposal' (1993) earned her the reputation of being a sex symbol. She even influenced fashion and thus, women of her time when she sported a short hair do, a pixie cut, on the red carpet of the premiere to 'Harry and Sally' (1989) that was soon channeled by both further celebrities and consequently women around the world (ibid.). Now, a woman with such a presence in public, acknowledged in the industry and influential, she had to fulfill expectations the audience certainly had towards her regarding her looks, her behavior, and certainly her status as a celebrity. What the audience apparently did not expect was seeing her naked and pregnant on the cover of a magazine.

4.1 Some Things Changed

"It's hard to imagine now, but the portrait of Demi Moore nude and pregnant on the cover of *Vanity Fair* was truly scandalous in 1991. Scandalous in the sense of shocking and morally offensive to some people" (Leibovitz par. 2).

And people were shocked: as a letter to the editor in Stabile's essay reads, people's reactions ranged from disgust to rejection to cynicism (Stabile 190). Several points of sale refused to sell the issue at all, while others insisted on having it wrapped as if it were a porn magazine (Tavani par. 4). The editors and responsible people at the magazine, however, were both fully aware that the photo would break ground and expected heavy reactions. Nevertheless, even the publishing company's chairman fully supported the publication (ibid.). And in a way, their plan worked as the issue was seen by a 100mil. people, sparked tremendous interest and had an unprecedented level of attention (ibid. par. 4). By knowingly crossing a line with that picture, Leibovitz, Moore, and Brown started a process that would change the perception of the female pregnant body.

By deliberately taking a picture of a renowned sex symbol during the final trimester of her pregnancy and stage her in a glamourous, fashionable manner, Leibovitz intentionally broke the "anathema" (Lupton 1) of the female pregnant body. The invisible pregnant body ceased to exist with being pushed to the spotlight the way the photograph did. Demi Moore conveyed the impression that the pregnant body is beautiful in itself and that a mother-to-be is absolutely entitled to self-consciously put her body on display and thus, remain an individual that is more than a "vessel" or "carrier". By consciously deciding to first take the picture and afterwards allow the publication, Demi Moore managed to preserve her status of a sex symbol on the one hand, but on the other hand enhanced the range of what can be regarded as such (Doll 3). In O'Brien Hallstein Moore is quoted saying, that "it did seem to a little bit more permission to feel sexy, attractive when you're pregnant [...]" (86). I would even argue that the picture enabled women to overcome the historical paradigms of self-neglect and even self-abandonment to liberation from constraints of heteronomy.

The publication of the photo can be regarded as the initial spark that allowed women to regain ownership over the pregnant female body and comfort and self-confidence. And consequently, the perception of being both pregnant and sexy and – most importantly – no longer feeling awkward and subjected to surveillance was decreasingly tabooed. A new way of seeing and perceiving pregnant women, apart from the de-erotization of medical accounts (Nash 29), was being paved by the photo and its publication. Likewise, despite the initially dismissive reaction, the photo claimed recognition in the public reality for pregnant women and thus, a disengagement from former social norms and cultural constructions (as described beforehand) started to evolve. So, the picture contributed to a general view on pregnancy as being socially acceptable (Matthews and Wexler 199).

With the increasing number of celebrities posing naked and pregnant (Doll 2), the idea of what a "good" or "bad" mother is shifted. Women were still seen as being "good mothers" although they felt comfortable and as an individual (Gow 7). Furthermore, the pregnant body no longer was regarded as an aesthetic problem (Nash 27) with body hugging maternity wear soon after the publication available (Leibovitz par. 2) and women having the assurance that the pregnant body no longer needed to be covered (O'Brien Hallstein 86) or as MSNBC's article puts it "pregnancy, in short, has become hipper, more glamourous – even sexy." (MSNBC par. 2). Interestingly, Leibovitz, as she claims herself, never intended to start this process but she feels "it's gratifying to think that the picture helped make pregnant women feel less awkward or embarrassed about their bodies." (Leibovitz par. 3).

4.2 Some Things Remained Problematic

The photo was published in a magazine that participated and still participates in the cultural construction of the ideal body as being slender and slim, putting the pregnant body in the "newfound focus" of tabloids (O'Brien Hallstein 85). So, in a culture that has a high appreciation of thinness, reading it as "a symbol for self-containment" (Nash 30) the depiction of a swollen, white belly had to clash. Furthermore, the physical female body continued to be "spectacles to the gaze of men" (Van Zoonen in Lowe 17). This requires the female body to be considerably smaller than the male body, "demure and take up little space" (Bartky in Giovanelli and Ostertag 2) making voluminous bodies the contrary of "appropriately female" (ibid.). Accordingly, it appears as if only those celebrities followed in Demi Moore's footsteps who seemingly were able to 'preserve' the pre-baby appearance to the greatest possible extent. Thus, Vanity Fair's issue reconfigured the cultural opinion on pregnancy (Nash in O'Brien Hallstein 85). This selected depiction goes along with the remnants of the attitude towards the pregnant body before the photo was published in 1991. A remainder of the disgust and the wish for invisibility and the alleged absence of sexual desires and attraction could still be detected. As a consequence, women were confronted yet again with idealized depictions increasing the pressure to physically achieve newly defined social ideals and "stylized images of the body", which have been rapidly spread by media (Featherstone in Lowe 19). It does not come as a surprise that Gow's study revealed the negative connotation with reports on weight gain during pregnancy (173). In combination with the effect that the maternal body was decreasingly perceived as a private matter, new performances of both poles (good and bad) occurred in the discourse (Nash in O'Brien Hallstein 87). The consequences will be discussed in chapters 5.2 and 5.3.

On the opposite end to the aspect of the idealized body women were and are still made responsible for the well-being of their pre-born. Even more so, as on the one hand, women increasingly became active in the decisions concerning pregnancy and birth (Lupton 3) while on the other hand, medical technology advanced to de-mystify pregnancy and yet again, put a monopole at third parties' hands, mainly doctors, to monitor the fetus' development (Stabile 194). Therefore, women could not evade the aspect of heteronomy fully. In order to comply with the social norms of being a "good mother", a goal increasingly difficult to achieve on the side of nurturing, women started to manage their bodies even before the actual conception (Lupton 3), to an extent that seemed like "reproductive asceticism" (Ettore in Lupton 3). So yet again, women feel obliged to control and limit their lives by constraining everything that could possibly harm the future foetus. Women still adhere to society's expectations of being a "good mother" requiring self-confinement and even self-neglect.

5   Where Are Pregnant Women Today?

Indeed, the developments triggered by Annie Leibovitz's photo lead to a new view on the maternal body, allowing expecting mothers to step out of the extrinsic obligation to 'curtain' their bodies. Moreover, women obtained a new self-consciousness along with body-consciousness, feeling no longer as a source for disgust but being allowed to feel sexy and attractive. Hence, the photo helped to de-stigmatize the condition of pregnancy from being awkward and vast. But on the other hand, the photo also put the maternal body in the spotlight of media and its evaluation. Ever since Vanity Fair featured that picture on its title, celebrity pregnancies were increasingly covered by media constructing an altered cultural view on the pregnant body as aforementioned. But with the growing media attention, this new view also affected the Average Jane[3]. Firstly, because she is encouraged to participate in the evaluation of celebrity pregnancies offered by the glossy (and even not so glossy) magazines. But secondly, she is also inclined to compare herself to the women featured and assessed (Gow et al. 173). The latter had a huge effect on pregnant women, striving to emulate the picture created by the media and thus, to conform with the new cultural image of the pregnant body. Furthermore, women feel almost compelled to "view themselves as sexual objects" during a phase, which should be dominated by other priorities than the "outsider's standard of attractiveness" (Fredrickson and Roberts in Gow et al. 172). This development's consequences a subject of the following paragraphs.

---

[3] Average Jane as a synonym for common, non-famous, and average women

5.1 Pregnancy and Media Today

The increasing media coverage of celebrity pregnancies has put the topic in complete media focus with high sales for those volumes featuring a story along with numerous images on an expecting celebrity (Doll par. 3). As Gow et al. point out in their study, celebrity magazines and websites have an enormous audience, e.g. the analyzed websites reached "13 million unique viewers" in 2007 to 2008 (172). As those reports and stories are dominated by images, the increasing exposure of pregnancy through media is strongly promoting the thin-ideal internalization among its audience, an effect even enforced by the trend of rather featuring already ideal-compliant models than other celebrities (ibid.). By reporting on the positive (or allegedly absent negative effects) of pregnancy only, as the "maternity glow" or the ease with which this phase passed through, magazines "cloud" the usual feelings of discomfort, weight-gain, or post-partum struggles (ibid.). By implying that the featured women are without any of those unpleasant side-effects and that pregnancy "is easy, natural, and enjoyable" (Hoffnung 164) magazines create an image of pregnancy that average women cannot fit in.

Moreover, magazines started to stress the competitive side of motherhood by comparing pregnant celebrities, as was the case in 2011 when both Kate Middleton and Kim Kardashian were expecting their first children (O'Brien Hallstein 87). By calling out the "battle of the bumps" and comparing the two women and the development of their pregnancies (ibid. 113), magazines introduced a new measure to assess pregnant women and the quality of their future motherhood. Not only served the choices of food or the likes of their cravings as an indicator for the quality of the future mom, but also choices of clothing, size of the bump, amount of weight gained and facial expression when being captured in pictures for the evaluation (naming Kate the clear winner by the way) (ibid. pp. 89 – 112). So, the women that were more coherent with the slender-pregnant ideal was the one assumed to be the better mother. Consequently, it seems as if society cannot get beyond the Victorian labels of maternal quality and the urge to subject women to external assessment, which now happens on grounds of appearance rather than on self-sacrifice and care. In fact, the underlying assumptions for what care is have changed from dedication and renunciation of own desires to body management and control, altering the former "ideology of 'good mothering'" (ibid. 18).

14

Another aspect of pregnancy in the media is the mutual benefit both the pregnant women and media are drawing from the coverage. Not only do sales increase considerably when a pregnant celebrity is featured, but also are the women exposing themselves boosting their level of fame on the one hand (Doll par. 3), while on the other hand they manage to keep their names in the public perception. And with the broad distribution of those stories, women's tendency to compare and contrast themselves (O'Brien Hallstein 15) to alleged role models is fueled. Their demand of channeling and mimic the presented examples led to a whole industry to evolve around pregnancy and maternity (MSNBC par. 11). Next to the change and increasing interest in maternity fashion, products like clay-prints from the bump, maternity beauty lines, and maternity photography evolved (ibid. par. 14). All those products were being designed after having identified maternity as a new market niche, which started to develop with the new take on pregnancy as a "special time" worth capturing (ibid. 11). This was initialized with Demi Moore's picture and further promoted by celebrities following suit, conveying the impression that "it's hip now to be pregnant" (ibid. 4).

Currently, it seems as if the pregnant belly has morphed into an accessory (Doll par. 3, O'Brien Hallstein 87). The (over)emphasis of the slender-pregnant ideal conveys the impression that women today have to be pregnant by belly only (O'Brien Hallstein 63) and unbelievably happy about it. Along with the change body-consciousness, the concealment of pregnancy struggles with celebrities, the slender-pregnant ideal creates a new kind of pressure on average women.

5.2 Having the Perfect Body – Throughout Pregnancy

"The public pregnant body [usually] resists or denies the monolithic and homogeneous images of impossibly slender women" (Nash 32) and potentially falling short with the physical appearance being the aspect by which women are assessed (Lowe 54). And whilst media has created a "template of slender-pregnant celebrity moms" in observing the likes of Kate Middleton (O'Brien Hallstein 63), women picked up the message and interpreted it as being their duty to be shaped and fit during pregnancy. Due to the "still voyeuristic 'male gaze'" (Lowe 50), women subconsciously enhance they attractive physical appearance throughout pregnancy and start to work out, even beyond a scope that is recommended by physicians, as I will later discuss. Generally, working out has obtained the notion of "good future mothering via restrained [...] choices, [...] and body management, especially via disciplined and controlled eating and weight management." (O'Brien Hallstein 63). So only if women conduct good body management they are likely capable of being good mothers. However, the slender-pregnancy ideal clashes with the image of the pregnant body being fragile and incongruous, only capable of " light strolls" (Jette in O'Brien Hallstein 90) but with the requirement of body management and control, work outs became inevitable, with scientists recommending that moderate exercises are safe for mother and baby (ibid.), linking it with easier birth and quicker post-partum recovery. Furthermore, with the association of slenderness with composure, the maternal body, which was initially seen as 'out of control', even more than the female body in general, the "contemporary maternal body norm" requires women to fully control their body throughout pregnancy in order to comply with this new norm (ibid. pp. 91, 94).

Recently, several women had obtained fame by putting their perfectly trim pregnant bodies on display. Presumably, those women fully complied with the above described body norm and took it to a new extreme. Narins features 10 women who documented the development of their pregnancies while working out, from running a 10k being 6 months pregnant to lifting heavy weights at 39 weeks. All of those women are visibly proud of their barely-there bellies sporting well defined abs (see appendix 3 - 6). All of those women at the same time became 'famous' as their posts on social media went viral. And all of them stressed that they are already or will be "good mothers" (see Williams in Narins, No. 9) following (probably unknowingly) the cultural norm of being evaluated by their physical appearance (Lowe 54). This strict regimen of nutrition and work outs seems to be the advancement of the before mentioned 'reproductive asceticism'. Knowingly, these women put their pictures only to be evaluated and judged. More than anywhere else, media's function as a panopticon becomes evident with these women's posts on social media. According to Foucault's theory of panopticism a system of surveillance and social control is in place persuading people to "control their behavior" in order to withstand the constant extrinsic observation and judgement (Giovanelli and Ostertag 1). In the case of women, even expecting women putting their maternal bodies on display, this links in with the idea of the male gaze and the women's feeling of urge to delight with their appearance accordingly. Hence, they comply with the evolved version of Foucault's panopticon, which initially was linked to the control of sex and crime, but in accordance with Bartky it today serves to encompass social media (Bartky in Giovanelli and Ostertag 1). Furthermore, this kind of social control has become "so pervasive in contemporary societies" that mass (social) media has become the central instrument to observe and control women's bodies (ibid.). As I have already lined out, media engages in relentless comparisons of pregnant celebrities and calling for competition among future mothers. Thus, women feel compelled to aim for the ideal body conveyed by such coverage in order to comply with the requirements of being a good mother. In a way, the picture of Demi Moore boosted that presumably ever present topic and catapulted it from the private to the public sphere.

However, it might be a little myopic to only trace the development back to the publication of the photograph. Additionally, women take a major part in this increasingly present and constant assessment. As Foucault puts it, it is due to the docility of women that today magazines, celebrity websites, television, and social media obtain the function of a panopticon. Women seem to have thoroughly internalized the patriarchal beliefs infusing media (ibid.) and seek to please the 'male gaze' (Lowe 50). Consequently, women constantly judge themselves through men's eyes and take measurement according to men's criteria (Mulvey in Giovanelli and Ostertag 2). To achieve compliance, women's bodies need to be "docile" (Foucault in Giovanelli and Ostertag 2) which is essential to create "ideal feminine" bodies (Bartky in Giovanelli and Ostertag 2). Hence, women control their bodies in every possible aspect by "diet, exercise, posture, and movement" (ibid.). And although pregnancy has been and is to some extent excluded from that, the women working out and sporting six-pack abs join in in seeking to comply with these standards. Apparently, they attempt to maintain an ideal feminine body or win it back as soon after birth as possible, as the photos in the appendix imply (No. 5 and 6). As for their motives to put their bodies on display, I can only assume that they fear rejection, shame, and insults (ibid.) if they transgress the ideal. If that holds true, an aspect beyond this paper, the women's fears could be linked to the deeply entrenched perceptions of pregnancy as being disgusting, incompliant with the male gaze, and thus, a negative assessment of their maternal qualities could be the consequence.

But there is this other aspect of motherhood or future motherhood I already touched on several occasions: the responsibility of the unborn child's well-being and the expectation that a pregnant woman should dedicate every activity respecting this. Hence, as soon as the first six-pack mom-to-be had posted a picture of her trim and barely there bump, inviting the onlookers to judge her, the backlash set in accusing her of potentially harming her child (see Narins, No. 9 Rebecca Williams). So, although with regards to their bodies, these moms should be seen as good mothers the social norm of responsibility for the unborn child would rather refute or contradict this judgement.

5.3   The Pressure of the Perfect After-Baby- Body

As the aforementioned phenomenon of six-pack abs mothers already implied, women feel subjected to the expectation to lose weight after birth as soon as possible and return their bodies to pre-pregnancy shape. And again, it appears as if a photo picturing Demi Moore on Vanity Fair's cover has sparked this felt necessity.

Exactly 12 months after her iconic cover and 9 after having given birth, Demi Moore once again posed nude for Annie Leibovitz. Covered only in body paint, she put her flawless after-baby body on display (see appendix 7). In contrast to the pregnancy shot, Moore's body faces the camera with light coming directly from the front, leaving little room to hide any imperfections. Although lighting is dim around her waistline it is clearly visible that her body is in excellent shape or, as Moore herself puts it, "looking better than in a bikini in [her movie] *Blame it on Rio*" 9 years earlier (Stage par. 9). As was the case with the first photo, this photo triggered a development no less interesting than the observation of a celebrity pregnancy. Media are lurking on how soon the new mother's body returns to its pre-pregnancy or even improved shape (O'Brien Hallstein 13) and celebrities seem to take this watch in. Accordingly, along with the impression of the easy and hip aspect of being pregnant, celebrities and the stories about them, all of which come with numerous pictures, convey the impression as if a pregnancy is something they can easily "slip in and out of, [...] a bump in the road" (ibid.). According to Waverman, this has not been the case in the 1970s or 1980s as she claims that women were not expected to lose their baby weight and get their pre-baby body back quasi immediately after birth, putting additional pressure on new moms (Waverman par. 18).

But seemingly in line with the argument of the panopticon and the constant judgement along with the desire to comply with the ideal feminine body standard, women again subdue to the patriarchal views and control their bodies. Again, I can only assume that they do this to avoid insults, body shaming, and social recognition as well as the positive evaluation of their maternal qualities.

6 Conclusion

In bringing this paper to a conclusion, it is necessary to look back at the initial thesis claiming that the photograph and its publication had positive as well as less positive effects. While on the one hand the picture is held jointly responsible for women and society to change their views ad perception on pregnancy and the pregnant body achieving a seeming liberation from former degradation to a passive entity, on the other hand, the publication caused to an objectification of the maternal body that had been mainly a private matter before.

The first aspect was to retrace the former views on pregnancy and motherhood stemming from the Victorian age enabling an understanding of the intense reaction the publication triggered. Throughout centuries, motherhood and maternity were subject to cultural rules and norms, which also served base for assessment of women and their mothering qualities. The construction of the gendered role reduced women to passive entities whose main task was to nurture and care, claiming this to be every woman's desire and fulfillment. Furthermore, women were thus coerced to abide by patriarchal norms, subduing to the perception of being a pathological condition requiring monitoring and control. Alongside, women were no longer entitled to individuality and personal needs and desires, morphing motherhood in to a constant state of self-neglect. The Victorian view of a woman being an ideal citizen when reproductive summarizes the understanding of the female role during that time.

In the course of time only minor changes took place, enhancing the societal expectation towards mothers by the aspects of appearance and positive self-perception. Pregnancy still was seen as a mostly private matter as the maternal body did not comply with the norms in place. Especially during the 1970s and 1980s, when the slim or slender ideal was coined, the pregnant body was expected to be kept out of sight and 'curtained'. Furthermore, pregnancy was still perceived as a reminder of sexual activity. With the pregnant body being subject to surveillance already during Victorian times, the level of heteronomy has further increased along with technical advancements in medicine, leading to a dispossession of the female body and hence, to women's individuality. Monitoring, medical advice, and extrinsic assessment oust women of their right to bodily self-determination.

Demi Moore's picture clearly contradicted the views on the maternal body as rebarbative putting her body self-consciously on display. And, with Annie Leibovitz intentionally juxtaposing this photo to the traditional views and constraints in connection with pregnancy and the pregnant body, she broke the anathema. At the same time, the publication made pregnancy a public matter even a public spectacle. By paving the way to make pregnancy a public topic, the publication helped to liberate women from the stigmata of pregnancy and partly of the heteronomy, with conveying that pregnancy as such and the pregnant body are no longer afflicted with shame and disgust but with positive coenesthesia. Simultaneously, with involving the media as the central medium of communication, this publication also triggered and enabled new means of control. It allowed the male infused standards in media to extend their sphere of influence to the once private phase of pregnancy and the delight of the male gaze. Furthermore, media initiated the competitive aspect of motherhood by redefining maternal quality from hardly measureable aspects like nurturing and care to measureable aspects of looks, including clothing and weight gain along with nutrition, and general behavior linked to body management and pregnancy. With media being a panopticon, women attempt to comply with those new norms and cultural ideals. An effect further intensified by celebrity moms who through the media focus make pregnancy seem more like a fashion item and 'easy business' and hence, increase the pressure on average women, who try to cope with ever new extremes of body control.

As a result, what seemed as being a step towards liberation from the culturally constructed corset, which it shortly and surely had been, the publication of the photographs discussed in this paper rather lead to an even more intensive form of self-control, which now appears to be voluntarily self-inflicted rather than imposed on women. But the voluntariness can be seen as specious as women cannot evade cultural expectation of maternal quality and its assessment. Likewise, the aspect of maternal responsibility cannot be overcome as future mothers, as much as they would like to feel and be seen as an individual, simply are not solely responsible for themselves during those 40 weeks, they always will also be responsible for the unborn child.

In the end, the course of the paper has shown that pregnancy has moved to the public sphere and changed the view on it to a liberal, less restrictive one with regards to body dislplay and motherly self-perception but at the same time, it facilitated new means of control and restrictions for future mothers to an extent that goes beyond the traditional constraints. So it sparked a change from heteronomy to a short phase of liberation to turn into an internalization of the extrinsic forces leading to self-inflicted total self-control.

References

Bellafante, Gina. "ART: What Celebrities Look Like: The Annie Leibovitz Aesthetic." *The New York Times.* The New York Times Company, October 26, 2003, http://www.nytimes.com/2003/10/26/books/art-what-celebrity-looks-like-the-annie-leibovitz-aesthetic.html, retrieved August 8, 2017.

Birns, Beverly and Dale F. Hay (eds.). *The Different Faces of Motherhood*, London and New York: Plenum Press, 1988.

Birns, Beverly and Niza ben-Her. "Psychoanalysis Constructs Motherhood". *The Different Faces of Motherhood,* edited by Beverly Birns and Dale F. Hays, Plenum Press, 1988, pp. 47 – 70.

"Biography for Demi Moore". *IMDb.com, Inc.* http://www.imdb.com/name/nm0000193/bio, Retrieved August 8, 2017.

"Biography for Annie Leibovitz." *Biography.com.* The A&E Television Networks, January 7, 2016. Web https://www.biography.com/people/annie-leibovitz-9542372. Retrieved August 8, 2017.

Davidoff, Leonore. "Regarding Some 'Old Husbands' Tales': Public and Private in Feminist History". *Feminism in the Public and the Private.* Edited by Joan B. Landes, Oxford UP, 1998, pp. 164 – 194.

Doll, Jen. "Let's Retire Demi Moore's Famous Pregnancy Pose Once and For All". *The Antlantic*, March 7, 2012.

Freeman, J. *Women: A Feminist Perspective*, Palo Alto: Mayfield Publishing, 1989.

Giovanelli, Dina and Stephen Ostertag. "Controlling the Body: Media Representations, Body Size and Self-Discipline". *The Fat Studies Reader.* Edited by Esther Rothblum and Sondra Solovay, NYU Press, 2009. Web https://www.researchgate.net/publication/280300549, retrieved on August 4, 2017.

Gow, Rachel W. et al. "Representations of Celebrities' Weight and Shape during Pregnancy and Postpartum: A Content Analysis of Three Entertainment Magazine Websites." *Body image* 9.1 (2012): 172–175. *PMC.* Web. August 6, 2017.

Hoffnung, M. "Motherhood: A Contemporary Conflict". *Women: A Feminist Perspective.* Edited by J. Freeman, Mayfield Publishing, 1989, pp. 157 – 175.

Landes, Joan B. *Feminism in the Public and the Private.* Oxford and New York: Oxford UP, 1998.

Leibovitz, Annie. "Annie gets Her Shot!". *Vanity Fair*, Sept. 2008.

Lowe, Miriam. "Research Into the Representation of Gender and Body Image in the Press - A Visual and Textual Analysis Examining the Presentation, Portrayal and Treatment of Gender and Body Image in British National Daily Newspapers". *School of Media and Communication, Faculty of Arts , Humanities, and Cultures, University of Leeds,* May 2012, http://media.leeds.ac.uk/files/2012/05/miriam-lowe.pdf. Accessed July 31, 2017.

Lupton, Deborah. *Configuring Maternal, Preborn, and Infant Embodiment.* Sydney Health & Society Group Working Paper No. 2. Sydney: Sydney Health & Society Group, 2012.

Matthews, Sandra and Laura Wexler. *Pregnant pictures.* London, Routledge, 2000. p.

McGuigan, Cathleen. "Through Her Lens." Newsweek Magazine. October 1, 2006, http://www.newsweek.com/through-her-lens-111991. Retrieved August 8, 2017.

Narins, Elizabeth. "10 Women Who Proved You Can Have Six-Pack Abs While Being Pregnant. They Redefine What It Means To Be a Strong Mom." Cosmopolitan, October 3, 2016. Online: http://www.cosmopolitan.com/health-fitness/a4463846/six-pack-moms/, accessed 08/14/2017.

Nash, Meredith. "Oh Baby, Baby: (Un)veiling Britney Spears' Pregnant Body". Michigan Feminist Studies, Volume 19, Fall 2005 – Spring 2006, pp. 27 – 49.

Neff, Christine L. "Woman, Womb, and Bodily Integrity". *Yale Journal of Law and Feminism*, Volume 3, Issue 2, Article 6, 1990, pp. 327 – 351.

O'Brien Hallstein, Lynn. *Bikini-Ready Moms, Celebrity Profiles, Motherhood, and the Body.* Albany: State University of New York, 2015.

Poovey, Mary. *Uneven Development: The Ideological Work of Gender in Mid-Victorian England*, Chicago: The U of Chicago P, 1989.

Robinson, Gail E. and Donna E. Stewart. "Motivation for Motherhood and the Experience of Pregnancy". *Canadian Journal of Psychiatry*, Volume 34, No. 9, December 1989, pp. 861 – 866.

Rothblum, Esther and Sondra Solovay *The Fat Studies Reader*. New York: NYU Press, 2009.

Shanner, Laura. "Reproduction". *A Companion to Gender Studies*, London: Wiley-Blackwell, 2004, pp. 405 – 415.

Siegel, Paul. *Communication Law in America*. London, New York, et al.: Rowman & Littlefield Publishers, 2nd edition, 2008.

Stabile, Carol A. "Shooting the Mother: Fetal Photography and the Politics of Disappearance". *Camera Obscura,* January 28, 1992, pp. 178 – 205.

Stage, Jeff. "Ms. Moore: Demi, Not Demure". *Syracuse Herald-Journal,* August 19, 1992. Web http://infoweb.newsbank.com/resources/doc/nb/news/0EFEEBBB2C8C5D52?p=AWNB. Retrieved August 15, 2017.

Tavani, Andrew. "1991 Vanity Fair Cover Featuring Pregnant Demi Moore Named #1 of Most Influential Images of All Time". New York Times, November 18, 2016. Web http://nytlive.nytimes.com/womenintheworld/2016/11/18/1991-vanity-fair-cover-featuring-pregnant-demi-moore-named-1-of-most-influential-images-of-all-time/. Retrieved July 10, 2017.

Waverman, Deborah. "Being Pregnant: Then vs. Now." Today's Parents. Rogers Digital Media, https://www.todaysparent.com/blogs/being-pregnant-then-vs-now/. Retrieved August 7, 2017.

"Celebrities make pregnancy seem glamorous". MSNBC. April 26, 2006. Retrieved July, 11th 2017

Picture References

Alexis, Sia. *18 hrs post-partum*. Diary of a Fit Mommy. December 10, 2014. Web http://fitmommydiaries.blogspot.de/2014/12/body-after-baby-it-can-be-done.html. Retrieved August 17, 2017.

Chelseapb. No title. Black Girl With Long Hair. January 4, 2017. Web http://blackgirllonghair.com/2017/01/6-black-moms-who-are-documenting-their-remarkable-pregnancy-and-post-baby-fitness-journeys-on-instagram/. Retrieved August 17, 2017.

Duncan, Chontel. No Name. Chontelduncan@Instagramm. March 23, 2016. Web https://www.instagram.com/chontelduncan/. Retrieved August 17, 2017.

Leibovitz, Annie. *Cover Vanity Fair, Issue August 1991*. Digital print, 1991.

Leibovitz, Annie. *Cover Vanity Fair, Issue August 1992*. Digital print, 1992.

Narins, Elizabeth. *Collage six-pack abs moms*. Cosmopolitan, October 3, 2016. Web http://www.cosmopolitan.com/health-fitness/a4463846/six-pack-moms. Retrieved August 17, 2017.

Appendix

1

(Leibovitz 1991)

2

ANNIE GETS HER SHOT
BY
ANNIE LEIBOVITZ

SEPTEMBER 8, 2008 12:00 AM

https://www.vanityfair.com/news/2008/10/annie_excerpt200810

Text removed due to copyright reasons

3

Removed due to copyright reasons

4

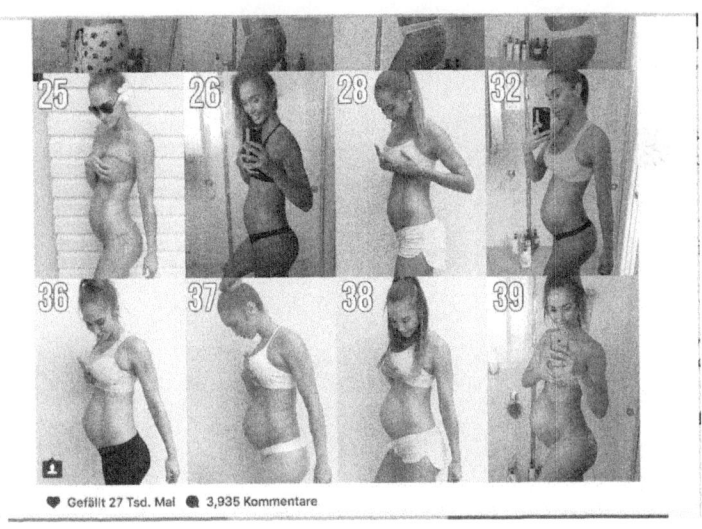

Gefällt 27 Tsd. Mal   3,935 Kommentare

(Chontel Duncan 2016)

5

(Alexis 2014)

6

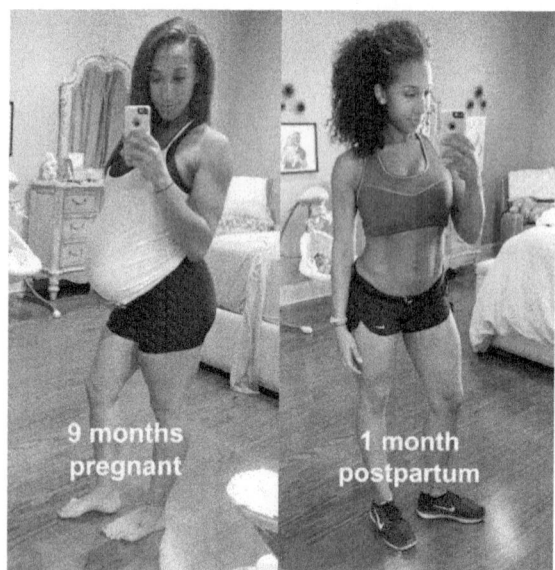

(Chelseapb@Instagramm 2017).

(Leibovitz 1992)